Nobody
Danced
With
Miss
Rodeo

OTHER BOOKS BY SID MARTY

Headwaters, *1973* (poetry)
Men for the Mountains, *1978* (non-fiction)

SID MARTY

Nobody Danced With Miss Rodeo

McCLELLAND AND STEWART

The Canadian Publishers
McClelland and Stewart Limited
25 Hollinger Road
Toronto M4B 3G2

Canadian Cataloguing in Publication Data

Marty, Sid, 1944-
  Nobody danced with Miss Rodeo

Poems.
ISBN 0-7710-5861-6

I. Title.

PS8576.A78N62   C811'.54   C81-094221-6
PR9199.3.M39N62

Printed and bound in Canada
by John Deyell Company

For Myrna, a girl of the golden west

CONTENTS

In the window of this back-alley atelier sits my raucous muse, the fattest magpie in Canada. Above its head the mountains rise for a long time, refusing to be upstaged. Yesterday in this town, where money turns over like hotcakes on a griddle, there was a restaurant called Great Expectations. The cowboys and Indians, tourists and mountaineers, husbands and wives in this book have great expectations, too; some that fall flatter than the sagebrush prairie where I was raised, some that still soar over the mountains on the margin of their lives. Narrow with death, big with love, let them move and go. "The stories are either true," croaked the muse, "or they are lies told by the characters." For, like my friend Al once said to me, "Unlike you, I no longer think of myself in heroic terms," and if the restaurant is still there tomorrow, I'll drink to that.

Sid Marty
Banff, January 1981

I
The
Spur

WHEN I JOINED THE OUTFIT

When I joined the outfit
they issued me
a 30-30 lever action rifle
20 rusty bullets, binoculars
a saddle and a bridle

With two old
but foolkilling horses

And a log house
in which I found
a package of noodle soup
three Hudson's Bay blankets
and no maps
to tell me where to begin

The house was where
the roads stopped and
when I joined the outfit
they gave me

400 square miles
of rivers, lakes
glaciers, mountains

The key to all the gates
They said Lock them all
behind you, I

Had time to travel in
peace of mind

A LA CLAIRE FONTAINE

I

By the cabin sits a fountain,
made of a spruce butt
carved into a frowning
chieftain's face, hook nose
and flat ears hewed with a saddle-axe
into the native wood.

It would be corny
this cigar store nobility
anywhere but here

Where game trails snake
into still unnamed mountains
Where the charred bones of bison
lie only inches below the yellow cinquefoil.

No teepee rings dot the meadow now. . .
Just the odd nylon mountain tent
pitched by weekend mountainpersons.

Still, rain has weathered the marks
of steel. The waterpolished features shine
as if they had been lambent
in the tree itself, discovered
in the peeling of the bark.

A clear spring, capped
by the mass of wood
leaps from the stones beneath,
writhes through an augered tube
and jets from the open mouth.

From the mask of some prolific god.

I think that way about it,
stooping to drink each morning,
meeting a mouth issuing
between worlds, kissed
by cold wooden lips
where sweet crystals flood the tongue

Imagining the statue smiles on me,
having to smile myself, at the notion
(while wondering which
its maker had in mind).

Some days it gleams in shadows.
Black outriders of storm mount up
the ridge of Eon, overhead.

But at that mouth
I fill my pail,
hearing a quieter voice,
benevolent and underground
at Bryant Creek.

II

The sculptor — I guess I'd call him that —
was a warden here in the park
He carved other faces in the tree trunks
along the trail, fierce surprises
that made nervous backpackers
balk like packhorses
when they caught sight of those hollow-
faced braves in the shadows

When he was lonelier than usual, he carved
languorous women reclining in a root
or hewed their faces into the posts
of the marker signs
— the ones that pointed to town

He carved and carved and
might have got them right
with time enough
and a forest of materials
for a perfect, wooden lady

But it wasn't enough, or else
he wasn't bushed enough
not to long for mortal company

So every few months, he'd saddle up
for town, where friends were mostly
married now, respectable, or gone

Scrubbed, dressed up
in his goin'-to-Banff Stetson
he'd start in drinking to forget himself

His rawboned look was just too western
His life mocked the pretensions
of the self-assured college boys
who gathered there. Off duty bellhops
in their uniform of denim
(basking in the ripped off image
of the working cowboy they despised)

Alone, with the young of the great
middle class, he would talk to himself
in the intervals
between dream and event
as he did in the backcountry
Wound up roaring out the answers
to questions no one else could hear

The waiters threw him out at last
He'd crawl up to the street
from the Cascade's basement bar

Drinking'd only made him thirstier
to taste one earthly woman

just
one,
where the thousand-thighed summer
swivelled disdainfully past
as he grovelled at its feet

A worshipper of form
whose sharp irony was
in the presence of desire
to be mute
to only drool at beauty

From talking to mountains
bears and horses
he'd neglected sweeter discourse,
become a human dinosaur
stranded, speechless
in the Age of B.S.

And so one day this tongue-
tied desperado bit
a lady on the cheek

Of her matchless
innocently
        eloquent
             backside
The superintendent said
Mister, get packed.
You're transferred north
with the rest of the wolves. . .

Well, maybe thinking of those vast
and uncarved forests,
where every tree concealed
some knotheaded girlfriend
just waiting to be unveiled;
in that despair, he framed
his most articulate speech

Just four little words,
two pronouns, two verbs.
He threw his badge on the desk,
said goodbye to the horses
and hit the trail

The fountain's face is cracked,
the stream runs on.
Whatever he meant to say
time will demean
quite soon, in this unworthy medium

I can't get anyone in town
to issue paint and keep this rot out.
Anyway, tree carving's illegal
in Canada's national parks
(except when building ski lifts,
highways or motels,
in which case gentlemen feel free
to chisel with a chainsaw,
delve deep with a dozer blade)

As for his unsolicited works,
I piece what's left
together, when I can
against the work of ants,
time's arrows, wind and rain

On runs the stream
Channelled, but indifferent
I see

A wide river waits
below this little, narrow flow

His love of stopping time
with wood, is fading like a dream
His carvings?
Most were stolen

They're in cities, now.

THE SPUR

An overbearing wind
clawed and roared through the spruce

And a blue butterfly
fertilizing flowers
was blown off course
to cling on my hat

The year was 1975
but I was still riding a horse
— part time

The horse was a victim of its desires
would not comply with my gentle hands

Three times a jet plane flew over
Three times the wild horse threw me
into the cinquefoil shrub

This horse and I were thousands of feet
high up a mountain valley
where the stones among the flowers
are the tips of slowly rising mountains

Where the stones are sharp among the flowers

Where incongruity's palpable
plateaus announce themselves
draw blood

Now I had a pistol in my saddlebags
(tools of the trade)
but I had left the bullets at home

So in my humility, I took off my hat
tried to caress those translucent wings
ever so gently with one, bleeding finger

But reality had settled there
like the beginnings of fever

Like the ripples of a sonic boom

The horse shied
And I knew that my humility
was arrogance. No match
for the diaphanous disguise of beauty

And I spread my scarecrow wings
I crowed my fury to the wind

Then the horse went up in the air
and came down, up and down

But I taught him, with the spurs
what I had learned
I sat him till he stopped

Till he was trembling with fear
And I loved him, for his hatred
was pure, weightless and winged

So sure was I of him
that I thought I'd fly him home

That was several years ago
and maybe long before

My butterfly
had flown

TERRITORY

The marten rubs his scent against a stone
as men who live in wilderness
will wet the corners of the yard
A talisman against intruders they suspect
would otherwise tear down the doors

Everywhere the natural delineates itself
Even a pine tree will bomb you
with dead boughs when you bite it
with a chainsaw

Everything seems light out here, sometimes
like a magpie playing with a squirrel
But my eyes remember darkness

I've seen that bird pull living flesh
from the fly-galled back of a steer

Only the stupidest animals
cows and men
will let death ride them

And yesterday, Coyote came down
to the edge of the house
with a snow white ptarmigan
in his mouth

To laugh at me behind the glass
that protects nobody

SEARCH AND RESCUE

The seat belt is my amulet.
As I adjust its magic, my gut reminds me
I'm thirty-five. The bigger you are
the harder it is to hide. Learned that
as a boy in school. Never got away with anything
there, either. Your turn to go today, they said.
Maybe rescue, maybe recovery. He was alone
on the southeast face, Mount Rundle.
A hiker heard him yell, saw something falling.
Might have been rocks. . . . Go take a look.
Write if you find work.

Oh laugh.
With all I can do to save my own life
every day, still there's this fear, of showing fear.
Bred in the boy to ripen in the man

My partner knows it, reads it in my eyes
No need to talk about it any more
Our thoughts have coupled though our bodies
never touched. Death makes us closer
than soldiers in a war

Death's a friend, like our pilot
with the wise, old eyes

The humour in them nods
at our exclusive fear
The one we don't admit
and he will not deign to show
as the doors are closed, and we
are all together, alone.

Our turbine whines, insanely
our rotors cleave the wind, faster
faster one by one the vari-coloured lights
flash serpent's eyes beneath the pilot's fingers

Fingering the seat belt
I'm a shaman, a primitive
caught in whiteman's magic

Never to believe that men can fly
except in the imagination
My blood denies it

Who dressed me for this dance?
Surely this isn't me
in warrior's harness again
hung with metal
hammer, pitons, carabiners

When I was a boy, I used to climb

I clutch the first aid satchel in my lap
my medicine bundle, with its orange cross
check the gaudy yellow climbing rope
coiled like a snake beside me
And my boots loom, worn and alive
propped on the plastic body bag

Through all the diagrams
through all technique
I smell the body; mine

And little I care for the melodramatic mountaineer
lost where rocky gendarmes rear
to snatch the clouds from Rundle

Arrogance is his unknown deathwish
gravity his conquistador

Grant him life, or a clean fall:
not to be hung up like the last one
on a wall of limestone
unravelled on a hook of rock
plucked at by ravens.

Fair haired David of a thousand lives
How many times must you be pulled
from your rock
and pushed into myth?
Your passion tires out the eagles

One of the crawling legion
who must be facing death
to know they're still alive

Such a grandiose
pinching of the soul
Such a stench of ego

And yet the smell of peril fascinates
and draws us near
into a kind of kinship, human.

When I was a child, I used to fly
from my bed, and sail the room awake
When I was a boy, I used to climb

Now if I fall, my friends will come for me
And file my name beneath "Recoveries"

So now I'll think of rescue as a dream
I never pinch myself until it's over

Relax, the pilot shouts
I love sex too much to ever. . .
(last words drowned)

But the joker's in my pack
with the lunches and the compass

Some priest has taught me cards
taught me how to lose,
and the shaman's smile is hollow

Enough to know that men
will never fly
That I am the boy
who fell out of bed
the bitter passenger in me

Whose heavy bones once warned him
Who felt the laugh of gravity
shaking in his arms
and, trembling now,
can hear the rivets singing
the molecule's complaint

Though power strains its carbon leash
to overwhelm his doubtful, smouldering cells

But look!

In the rotor dust outside, a face
Another boy

Who watches openmouthed
with ardent, burning eyes

He presses the fence, half crouched
under our invisible sickle

I wave him back, but he stands his ground
Waiting for a sign
for the gate to open
to let him aboard our monster

Powered by the dark blood
of dinosaurs, the engines howl
There is no answer, but a mocking
echo, from gravity's splendid silent walls

He waits for recognition
in my eyes! He wants my place
or that I wave at least

His mini-god, his future self
rising in a whirlwind of dust

How can I confirm what I don't believe,
but how deny that look? Tell him
Boy, I merely spin toward nothing
at greater speed than you, tell him

Son, you are mistaken
we cannot fly

When he, with such unbearable certainty
waits for the great ship to sail him clear
of earth's motherloving hands

His desire is the wave
that launches us

I feel my arm float up
thumb raised, against my will
Betrayed, betraying
in the rotor's howl

The pilot's hand contracts
and gently flexes on
the ship's electric phallus

Slowly we lift, and rock toward the sun
Old earth grows strange, and far
through plexiglass and steel
I could step out in the air
go back to it
But now is real, is altitude
a barrier more tangible than these
My amulet keeps me still
enraptured by the tricks
with matter and arithmetic
that only humans do
(what bird need bother. . .)

Pilot, smiling pilot
save us once again
I know that men will never fly
But I'll suspend my disbelief
in this rush of power
seething through my veins

I know that boy
I've seen that look before

And now the mountain draws us close above
with windy breath, its larch trees yellowing
with autumn, below the precipice. We scan

We see through ages, miles of lifted time
The old horizons of an ancient sea
And there's the sign we're looking for

A crimson tear
that joins the broad, seamed intervals
On the icy face of love

THE YEAR IS ANY YEAR

The loud boats are quiet in the arms of the shore
And the sun is spent, blown out by an evening wind
Then the nighthawk whirls and dips like an invisible top
Plunged over the lake, and the fishermen are drunk
Too drunk to hear its whirling song

Dark horses gallop on the mountain trail
Their manes crackle; the thunder walks up there

The year is any year, for engines have gone to sleep
Only the new moon rides these shadowy deeps

SWAMP KING
for Perry

We thought he was a rogue black bear
A savage runt, the mauler of four:
one man blinded, one clawed up
one died later in the doctor's care

That was the worst,
and then the fourth man
shortcut the warning signs
that closed the swamp

In the dark willow bush
he met the bear head on
and crawled out, half scalped
over beaver dams to the road
With the blackrobed
Justice of the Peace
growling at his heels

"He was black, pure black!"

The Indians at Morley said he was a spirit bear
I think they prayed for him
They asked us for his body, for their rites.

Some thought he was senile
Some that he had a tapeworm
"Or maybe he's got a dead pilgrim in there
waiting for him to ripen"

And the summer help sat in the pubs
talking knowingly about imported bears
brought in to draw the tourists
A chamber of commerce plot

But the bear stayed in his swamp
and said nothing
It was his court
and the moves were all his

In the swamp the birds sang
oblivious to tragedy
The tracks of black bears
covered everything
There was a bear for every tree

Around the swamp, we stood with rifles
while snares were set, baited with beaver meat

The swamp went crazy, fighting for our offerings
And in the dark, the black bears came out, running,
like rabbits leaving a fire
First the little ones, then the large

Brief shadows between the headlights
No way to shoot, and a good thing, too.

For in the dark heart of willows
there was a cry
of unbearable sadness and fury

Next morning, in the snare
we found him
He was black, all right
A coal black grizzly
over 700 pounds
caught in the half-inch cable
by the right front foot

He'd carved a crater in the mud
with his free paw
Bit down trees eight inches through
waiting for us to come to him

Afterwards, measuring our pygmy hands
against his armoured foot
we said he was a gentle bear
because he pulled his punches
defending a hunting ground

Though when he came
for his executioners
beckoning them closer
with his five-inch-long claws

He hit his tether so hard
that the trees trembled in pain
and leaves fluttered to earth

He rolled with the bullet
in his skull
But stood up on his hind feet
up
and up
shaking his head
at the insult of that lead bee

Came down like a bomb
exploding in the flying dirt
toward the sound of shotguns

Holding his five front talons
out like supplicating, ivory fingers

Falling and getting up
Falling and getting up.

Science took the body
slung from a helicopter
swaying slowly in the breeze

One of the shooters clipped
his daggers for a necklace

The noise of the traffic
never stops, along that road
But after a while
the birds began to sing again

IN THE ARMS OF THE FAMILY

Once, in a metal dragonfly's belly,
deaf in a clamouring, flying
bomb of turbo fuel
I flew these valleys
My life hung
from one whirling blade
shaken
by the cross winds boiling
through these gap-toothed mountains
scoured by wolvish tongues of ice
ten thousand years ago

The hard winds lifted us
through gates of rock and cloud
the elk and the bighorns
running uphill away from us
out in the imagined quiet in
the unrolling of a silent film

How I strained to hold their reality!
Remembering sounds of hooves on stone
before my head dissolved,
washed through in the turbine's roar

Far below was boundary camp, my tent
where I'd lain awake those nights
listening for a poacher's horses
Making my living
with an ear to the ground
and waking with only the hum
of blood inside the brain

My thoughts turned to the life outside
as if the novel cities held solutions
far off and wonderful as dream,
places full with sounds of living

I sat there rattled by my fantasies
stomach hooked up on a cloud

Below Cascade I saw my home
half believing in a second I would plummet free
into the yard. I pitied those who love me
Trapped with their provider
in the chances of such work

The tools of the territory include
climbing ropes and helicopters
guns and dynamite

The risks are arithmetical
The search for the survivors never ends
or the inventive faults of the violent dead
Those brothers, grown up separate and strange

We tracked them to their shattered endings
and life became a minor war
in a blue theatre of mountains

Then once, checking for life
in a young man's staring pupil

I saw myself
at the bottom of the soul's well

And I knew
danger was my fix, too.
Needed to survive.

These high walls were home
because I saw them as they are
and asked for nothing but life

Yet in my climbing
never to arrive, to know
no summits but the skyrack
of a poem whose jagged edges
rule my head

When I was home, where I could rest
the voices of my woman and son
seemed like echoes heard by an eavesdropper

I had been listening for men,
and only heard the bear
that knocked my grub cache down

After the wind died
I thought I heard the sound
that flowers make
following the sun around

And then they came for me;
swept up by aluminum angels
borne forward in time
to listen here, for love again

But where are you, that reads?

Is it a high building
with rows of lights below,
or do you have your own
dark roads to listen to?

I can describe, if you'll accept
these jumps from death to life

That in a wilderness of one
we travel back and forth
where time is fiction

It's why I lose myself, sometimes
One who knocked the wind aside
and fell through mountains
like a skipped stone

Can't imagine he arrived safely
could be loved
for the merely human moment

which speaks for itself
to hush the vociferous buzz
of doubt

But he who was lost
will wake up found, and right

In the arms of the family
that binds him again, to his life

BIG GAME

Look how the elk move over that hill

They cut their lives in snow
above Cascade. Higher still, the bighorns go
daring the avalanche slopes

On the road, the skiers jockey
in their fast cars, the sons and daughters
of oil men, Calgarians. They hurry to encounter
ski lifts.

When the game comes down to water
to drink from the clear, blue Bow
in ranges cut by highways

They will die, one after another
beneath the wheels

In the paradise of the middle class

WHEN I LEFT

Twelve years rolled by
Not all of it was memorable
When I left the outfit, they
didn't ask me why.
I told them anyway

They gave me
a refund on my pension
eight months late, and
without interest
My old and bloodstained
climbing boots for a souvenir
They kept the rifle
the horses the cabin
and they changed the locks
(I think the packrats ate my blankets)

I left because they murdered
the peace that I had found

And handed me a photograph
of a mountain

II

Nobody Danced With Miss Rodeo

GREYHOUND

The drunks come to the depot when the night is cold. They dream
of leaving Calgary, of entering the pictures on the wall. Horses in a
field, clouds and mountains give them hope. They wait for the
squad cars to arrive, and watch the buses leave again without them.

You arrive too early, sit there
tasting the desperation and the smoke
trapped in schedules and promises again
On your left, an aging flower child
tells you he is "into farming now"
Thumbs through your book
of mountain poems, with critical fingers
(he has a Ph.D.). On your right, an Indian
slumps against your shoulder, drunk

You thought you were safe in your white skin
or just took it for granted (the same thing)
in this depot of greyhounds
So it bothered you a little —

But then the guard comes down
starts in shaking him, without effect
And you don't, suddenly, like
the goon's grimaces as he works
The swearing underneath his breath
is audible, done for your benefit
when you didn't ask for it

And you never liked security guards
the private exercise
of public power, so you say
Why don't you just leave him alone
he ain't bothering anybody

He straightens up, and damn the man
sneers at you behind his ferret eyes
his powder blue fake battledress

and struts toward the phone
as if he was some bigshot general
calling for air support
And not just a jazzed up
washroom attendant
calling the real police again

He dials the number
flashes you a patronizing smile
It washes out at you
like a ripple
on the surface of a slop pail

And you: you're only a token liberal
safe in your greyhound skin
No one makes you clean up the puke
or drag the comatose drunks to the wagon
But you let this drunk's head stay where it is
just the same
and he isn't your brother, and you are a fool

While the women who now begin
to resemble cows, the men
somehow taking on the masks
of baboons, pink-faced baboons
leer over the tops
of their *Midnight* magazines
Oh they make you feel so sleazy,
tacky, like a man in drag

Because the shade of aroused bovinity
darkens the human eye
while in the air the promise of blood
flares each titillated nostril

Enter this rednecked clodhopper, stage left
wearing a polyester leisure suit
safari cut, and a straw cowboy hat
perched on his round skull
like a beercap on a bowling ball

He looks at you and the guy you seem
to be necking with. I'm a good Indian,
he quips. One drink and I'm gone for the night
He sips his coffee and grins at his joke

You are the joke.

You smile your little smile, thinking
how violence seems so necessary
which is just death offering the brain logic
But you long to hammer that tiny hat
down over that wrinkled brow
with the back of your fist
and then maybe screw it down
a wrinkle or two, between your wrists
wanting things to fit better than they do

You glare at the sonofabitch
and try to remind yourself
last time you got in a fight
— two hours in emergency, chipped teeth
cauliflower ear and a broken writing hand

If he says one more word,
but then another drunk comes on, stage right
or cage right in this Greyhound zoo, says
I'll handle thish guy, and begins to
roughly shake your drunk and pull his ears

Maybe he's a relative you think
they are the same hue, but then you see
how craftily he eyes
the goon on the phone, who notices
and smiles. The crowd begins
to twitch and murmur. Galvanized
by some arcane energy

The drunk's head bangs on your shoulder
So to hell with this, you say at last
and get up, move away

Sick of your porridge-coloured skin
and your safety

The goon on the phone sees
you have come to your senses
gives you a welcoming smile
and you shy from that vacuum
like a colt skipping a badger hole

You stare at the wall instead
trying to read the schedule
but it's all a code you can't decipher
There is nowhere, yet, to go.

The sound of a blow arrests you.

The waker upper knows his audience
He's slapping the helpless face
with open-handed swipes.
The fascinated passengers edge closer
like children drawn to a magician

The heavy weight of their expectations
freezes you, in the mind not
of the matador, but the bull

In the parody of a boxer's dance
our magician holds the crowd.
He feels the bingo in his arteries
turning into wine. A miracle. And now
your drunk reels forward to his feet
reluctant player

Up comes a hand to shield his face
too slow. The punch is to the nose —
blood flying. Fight, you sonmuhbitch
the boxer cries, finding his audience
irresistible, he begins to believe
in himself again, but

Weaving, half asleep
or like a boy who doesn't understand
his father's anger, the drunk
shrinks back
from the hunger in that room

You hear the drunk's skull
hit the marble floor of the Greyhound depot
feel the shock in your brain
see the blind look of a cornered mammal
in the victim's eyes
try to shout something, hear
someone else say
That'll knock some sense inta him. . .

Even then, you couldn't move your feet.
It was the television cackle
of their laughter broke the spell
their taped response, their inability
for pitying that pulled you back,
animate again, in hatred

Such a long sad time, being human.
Because we have to act at last
if it takes us forever

What you did was wrong.
You should have played it safe
offered suggestions
and been a dead man, standing up

But with an angry moan, like a tricked animal
that has swallowed a sharpened bone
hidden in a bait, listening to nothing
but the pain inside yourself, you take
a slow motion mauling leap across the floor
as the boxer's fist comes back
for another blow

Jump through the laughter
tear your nerves on its hooks
your paws reach for the switches
in their throats to turn it off

You charge through the scarecrow boxer
a man made of sticks
hurt him more than was needed
send him flying into the crowd
as they back away

Stop laughing
you say, suddenly ashamed,
for them all, for yourself, too.
It isn't funny, you say, pleading.

But the sullen crowd is not convinced
Their faces turn opaque again, turn into chalk.

Now they edge past you
as if it had nothing to do with them
and it wasn't the blood of man that's smeared
on the floor of the Greyhound depot
spilled for their entertainment

The sirens are loud and too late outside
Time to get lost.

Well. You gave them quite a show
because like any fool
you think you know something
the crowd does not

The farmer gives you back
your book of poems, convinced.
You are no poet.

Forgive me if I still have doubts, myself;
it keeps you honest.

The buses roll out

NEWS

A newspaper floats above the world
held at arm's length on the wind
and on the red flowers, the yellow flowers
the black and white horses
go running over their hills

A kite is hurled sideways
Words are shouted down by the sun

Tattered, the sentences the phrases
drift to earth like prayer flags
held in the long-fingered grass
washed and eaten by time

THE RIFLE

In a pickup truck's back window
there is a rifle hanging
over the lives of three people
riding south to Kimberly

Low clouds and mists that day
Sudden runnels of light
play down mountains, shining
across their windows
upon this rifle

Its telescopic sight
is picked out by the sun
and flashes where the blueing's worn
to silver. The sight's a tunnel
Landscape rushes through it
in a blur of colour
no one sees. Blind pupil
recorder without a record

Coldly noted and forgotten
fence posts click by
a horse, a crow
a coyote, a man

A man is driving.
It must be his rifle.
He has hung it there above the heads
of his passengers: a blonde-haired child
staring backwards down the road,
a woman who never turns
to look at anything
a motionless figure

The child raises one hand to wave
The rifle barrel seems to arc
from right to left across the window
jerked by the flickering light

Motion interrupts its bright repose
Every line of it grows clear

And the muzzle now appears (but this
is probably a trick of light)
to rest against the woman's head

As it says above, a trick of light.
Or else why would she be content to ride
there, with her head filling those crosshairs

To be watched by a rifle
A tool for punching holes
through anything that lives

I'M SO LONESOME IN THE SADDLE SINCE MY HORSE DIED
for D.L.

"Well, he rode the bush rodeos.
He was sure enough a cowboy,
he was a hand.

God he was rank, though!
Always ridin' his horse through some bar,
such a tired old trick.

He done that in Cochrane.
Comes chargin' thru the pickups out front
and right through the front door.
And if he wasn't doin' it,
he was holdin' the door
for some other rangy-tang.

One time he rode in with his lariat —
roped guys right outta their chairs
skidded them into the parking lot like calves. . .

Boy they was hungry for him that day!
All them drugstore cowboys from Calgary,
chased him with trucks all over town
That horse jumpin' fences and
him duckin' clotheslines
with bedsheets and pantyhose
strung around his neck.
That was a pretty tame mount he had
that time, I tell yuh.

They call 'em 'urban cowboys' now,
yuh know. Shee-it!
Buncha drunken half-ton jockeys
all duded up in their Rexall regalia,
they couldn't cut 'im off,
just smashed each other up instead,
at every corner.
He made it to the river
and hid out in the trees.

48

Ain't it strange
how well some men can ride
yet never make good horsemen.
He treated horses like he hated 'em.

I disremember when it was
he bought this mighty gelding, Boots.
That pony really threw the honkytonk
on Jim, he could not stay aboard.

So he tripped old Boots
with a Scotch hobble.
Yuh know he kept that pony down
until its hooves came near
t' fallin' off.

I always suspicioned him to be
'bout two bricks short of a load
but that was a bit too western for me.

Old Boots was about ruined.
'Fox the sonmuhbitch then,'
says Jim.
'He'll make some dog sick.'
(He didn't like dogs, either)

His wife, though, she was a wonderful woman,
a big skookum girl from Spillamacheen
but a beauty.

Never asked for much, 'cept once.
She wanted a TV. Well, he bought her one
in town, threw it in the truck
and proceeds home, drunk
which was his rule
over Texas gates
at amazin' speeds. . .

Natchrally the set
got bucked into the tulies. . .
But he gathered up the remains

and when he got home
dumped this junk on the floor, says
'There's yer TV, hon.
It's a colour one, too.'

And he laughed, that fool.
Figured it was a helluva joke.

She never left him, though.
What a woman sees in a man like that,
I'll never know.

Guess he met his Waterloo
in the Caroline Hotel
— some big roughneck dismounted him real hard.
A month of hospital rations kinda tamed him down. . .

Next I heard, they'd moved to Utah.
Guess he was a bit ashamed of it all.
He was born too late, yuh see,
for the time he was livin'.

Like when we was ropin' cows,
he'd never wear gloves. . .
He says 'They never wore gloves, the old guys.'
Well jeez you know they couldn't afford 'em, probably!
His hands was like hamburger, but he'd say,
'The only thing yuh can do well with gloves on
is shit yer pants.'

He wouldn't even wrap the horn with rubber
to take the dallies. The old timers never
used that, either. 'Well you dipstick,'
I told him, 'they didn't have it to use, is why.'
All they had was that shaganappi, rawhide.

Then he'd tag some old bitch of a Hereford,
and he'd burn them hands, Lordy!
Make yuh cringe to see it. . .

Just a big stubborn kid all his days
Livin' in the past
he never knew,
gettin' it wrong all the time.

Maybe that's what it was
with her. Some women love a loser. . .

Anyway, he was sure enough
aw-thentic cowboy.

He was a hand."

NOBODY DANCED WITH MISS RODEO

And she was too dignified to hula-hula
with the heavy-thighed Hawaiian
dancing girls, entertaining the yokels
in a hockey rink turned beer garden
for Round Up Daze

Nobody danced with Miss Rodeo
in their ersatz Munich cum phony Waikiki
though they rushed the stage to don
fluorescent grass skirts
indulging a Treasure Island fantasy
forgetting the prairie
and its adult pain
free of the wind and the hail
wreathed in exotic leis
of polyurethane
bellies wobbling
the sons and daughters
of the pioneers
of every prairie nationality
had buried their differences
in one dance
the Swedepolukulelewaspgermanic polkahula
It would have thrilled to very jism
the minister of multiculturalism

Too bad he had declined the invite

O Rank Montanon!
Whiskey trading founder
of old Whoop-Up town
deeply buried beneath our pleasure
your skull must be
rattling in this din
like a lusty cash register

Miss Rodeo, demure, was not amused
Few cowboy hats were seen
(bobbing above the crowd
of local merchants)
to rally round the bright
red Stetson of their Queen

Most cowboys had been slightly
crocked up in the afternoon stampede
by bulls and broncs and whatnot
and drinking to ease the pain
were in no mood for hula-ing
and foola-ing around a hockey rink
this far east of Waikiki

In the middle of the hot
baldheaded prairie
The only cowboy hats flopped graceless
round the ears of rent-a-cops
descending on a sodbuster, who
undeterred by the grim
aura of fun
let out a rebel "Whoopee!" then
being of Gaelic stock
jumped on a table of beer
to dance the Highland fling
brandishing a jack-knife for a sword

Ah Miss Rodeo
I rose in pity to enquire
but froze, seeing in your eyes

Open range and water rights
Private schools in Switzerland
Sagebrush and contempt

With the image of a paraplegic
Cowboy Prince
crushed by the wing

of a bull named Airtime
a vanquished buckeroo
who's bumpersticker credo was
"I'm a lover, a fighter
and a wild bull rider"

But Miss Rodeo
surely you will recognize
a cowperson?
Peruse these Acme riding boots
elegantly trimmed in dung. . .

How can you partake, my Queen,
of this Kiwanis fantasy?
Let me chronicle your worth
among the bellowing herd
of homogenized Kanucks

I see your beauty
speechless in polyester
and I appreciate the stallion
parked outside
at the gate of disappearing mountains

So leave with me
and be my *leitmotif*, oh muse!

Miss Rodeo did not deign
to speak, but coolly followed me
out for a little *lebensraum*

Out where the boys were drinking whiskey
and quietly licking their wounds
wrapped in their jeans and glory

Old hands tune the fiddle and guitar
A hole in the clouds lets in the prairie stars

Miss Rodeo, their eyes light up
at your approach
"Pull up a beer case, ma'am
and set a spell"

Here are your few
your aching subjects
waiting for you to bless
their scars; waiting for you
to judge their stories

SEX ACTS WITH BEASTS

Ants, I have read, milk aphids
like the tiny green ones in that tree
raining their sticky exhalations
insect ecstasies onto my head
until I'm coated with their microscopic bliss

I can almost hear the whirring of antennae
hosannas of the leaves, as I lie beneath the boughs
reading Kosinski
Unnatural acts, whips; a girl with a goat

A woman I know told me
riding horseback in summer heat
brings her to the point of orgasm
And by now
she may have overcome a slight repulsion
and given her horse free rein, so to speak

I've sometimes wondered about women on stallions
remembering the tale of the Russian empress
who decided to get under instead of on

Her block and tackle broke
in flagrante delicto
and she wound up wearing the horse
You might say the horse
had a crush on her, too

Far fetched?
I thought so.
Even a queen's libido
must have its limits

But then I heard about the other extreme
A farmer, caught by the police
committing an act most foul
with a chicken

"Well, you see, your lordship, he'd take
the hen into his livingroom and pour them
a drink, then one thing would lead to another
and he'd, uh, well he, uh. . . "

Technique, technique!
This country worships diagrams

The part I can't figure is
how in hell did the cops find out
about this chicken seducer
out on the farm. Was he bragging in town
about his conquests?

It's bad enough, the Mounties opening our mail
Next they'll be sneaking around
the goldurn henhouse armed with catheters
prying into every good-looking pullet

Come busting in with a search warrant. . .
"Just keep your hands flat on the table, fellah.
Corporal Basher — check the pedigree on that omelet. . . "

The media bombards us with advice
How to build the perfect sex life
with elevations, front and rear

Total strangers hunger to confess
acts of unbridled lubricity
It really brings the puritan out in me
to see our wholesome horniness
praised into jaded stupidity

And the birds with the bees do dally
in the lustful honeycomb
The girls in their seasons come
and go. Then the lonely afternoons
with books of strange scenarios, when
too little is more than enough

Like these aphids
fondled by ants
too much

When sex rains down from heaven
sometimes it feels like hell
Its kiss a thousand tiny spiders
on the skin

Get up, go into any room
and close the door

THERE WAS A LADY MET A BEAR
(in Jasper National Park)

There was a lady met a bear
The lady, wearing cold cream
Was lying naked in a tent
Beside a mountain stream

This lady had a sunburn, and
I should have said before
How really terrified she was
When the bear came through her door

So quietly, on padded feet
With expression somewhat bored

There must be fats in cold cream
and oils that black bears love
— Someone should do a study
Though I don't know what it'd prove

Perhaps it's high in protein too
— I really do not know
But the black bear licked the lady
In her tent, so cool and shady
The black bear licked the lady
From her head down to her toes

The lady didn't scream, oh no
But, terrified, lay still
Trembling 'neath the black bear's tongue
It was pink and insatiable

And when the black bear ambled off
She dressed, got in her car
And hurried to the nearby town
To buy another jar

THE WEIGHTLIFTER

Charles Noble, the poet
lifts weights in the afternoon

He curls a hundred pounds
of iron in one fist, twisting a barbell
ponderously from the floor
up
to the tip of his chin
and sits considering it
in philosophic pain

Charles Noble, whose name
is taken seriously
in Nobleford, Alberta
(where the Nobles are nobility)

Has learned to prefer
anonymity
to fame

He lives in Banff
drinks cases of beer and growls
ideas and belligerent rhymes
at friends and enemies alike

Redbearded, leonine, he drinks
and studies poetry
in a solitary basement room

His grandfather invented
a cultivator blade so famous
that the wheat remembers and dreams
of tumbling under the curl of black loam

This plough, this blade
lives on in Noble's wrists now
        a dumbbell
        voiceless idea

a single note he wrestles
back to life, these winter nights

As if he could ever wring from it
the child, the man, his body and soul
transformed by love and blood alone

This Noble might quiet the wheat
if he chose. With verses rustling out
of his feathery beard
in one deep chorus, like snow

For the land is in Noble, who lives in town
It won't let him forget the crocuses
or the dead crows, stiff-legged cows
in swollen creeks, meadowlarks
their inevitable roistering
at the flashy weathercocks, free of winter
flying away with the unpainted barns

While combines dream of forges and heat
rivulets of sweat and the longed for blood
to oil the rusty tongues of metal
And earth's dry body strains beneath
the loving hands that are mortgaged

The plough surrenders at last, for a time
snow blows against the pane

Noble lifts it up exhausted, ecstatic
across his chest in the brightening window

DEATHSONG FOR NELSON SMALL LEGS jr.

I

The poem of your death grows
and the politics it touches now
will be contained within its motion

So the deer eludes the arrow
but not the eye, the mind
that drew the bow
or the imperfect heart
that follows it, weighted
with all your hopes

Death was your last art.
Whether it was the fool's fantasy
sublime whim
or the act of a desperate hand,
it will not be confined by these

The song of your death is a brook
widening from the bottom
                        of the reservoir
For power, too, is temporary
though the powerful sit behind locks
dreaming of clocks and interest and
                        clockwork lust
The report unnoticed on their desks
until it suddenly grows fangs and strikes

Too late! Already the roots
of a thousand trees are watered
and the bloom spreads down
the mountain to the valley

A wave of colour regards the day.
It plunges down the canyons of the dead
it harrows their bones from the niches
and paints the cities of its rainbow green again

II

Of your life you once said
"It's good to be up here
walking that knife edge"

Yet always the temptation to fly
catches those who love the earth
because they want to hold it all
at once in their eyes
and bury it in the heart

The arrow has flown from the bow
lead from a trigger, flew.
The goat jumps from ledge to ledge
to meet the predatory eagle

Love weaves its nets for catching souls
if such a net could ever be that strong.
Its threads are foolish, desperate and sublime
and the colours come of a weak human dye

The song of your death sings on.
Moans in the building tension of wires
strung across rock and prairie
shivering in the pipeline and the railway
until the light of the eye turns on them
to show the skeleton of the body politic
a haywire X-ray, a blueprint of its death

Unknown yet, the frame of rock
Unknown yet, the purposes of root
                              and branch
Unseen still, the flower under the skin
that everyone, anyone, felt stirring once
in the voice of a friend

Nelson, tell us why.
All I can argue is "All flesh is grass"
I never knew you, and they'll think
I speak of Indians, yet

The rock of your desire will remain
with your soul of root and branch

The kiss that never died
passed on from man
to woman, to man. The gift of your life

Which you sang to this world
before you lay down on the wind
of history, and died

Leaving us our barbaric sorrow
Leaving us adrift on your blood

THE HUNTER

Maybe looking at a dead bird
in your hand, you think
it is a metaphor of autumn
for you appreciate the symbols
and the burning bush of the seasons
You know what you represent
as you throw it in the bag
there with the others, dead

Their throats are stuffed with rose hips
they have gathered in the coulees
for all the land is bleeding
and the pyres of the year are smoking

Maybe you remember, how like a baby
a plucked bird looks
All beasts look the same
under their thin veneer

But the land is under your feet
and you have the means to reach
into the sky, so you go on gathering
the birds out of the air

Those that are crippled
are timid in the grass
They are beautiful
as you take them up

To feel their captive wings
trembling in your heavy hands

ON A BUS NEAR SALMON ARM

Grey head looking from the window of a bus
Grey mists swirling down the Shuswap
Dog legged corners, log fenced orchards
Built by a young man
many memories ago

Black and white is the road, it's sure
And black is the raven of certainty
A shadow in the yellow leaves of autumn
and like autumn, promising
only winter

Grey haired the mountain, streaked with snow
The old lady, head full of dreams at her window
Black is the raven
the snow rides his wing

AT CRAIGELLACHIE

At Craigellachie a phallic tower of stone
remarks each locomotive horn since men drove steel
through these scarred canyons

Drove steel, and where
(we now would wonder)
did women hide
from history's eye
But we know that they were
everything, behind and forward
of that line

Love more than pride
drove the muscle in the arms
that swung the hammers down
(Pride relents)

Wind in the trees, the passage sings
of survey gangs and starving horses
of powder monkeys blown to bits
while tamping nitro with a crowbar
Bad jokes were the pride of the builders
pride of men
(Love endures)

Across the China Sea
or Galway, in the famines
were women who had lost their men
women who sent blood
to grease the rails in Canada
and waited for the last spike
to be driven, in their hearts

Their grief, the cry of steel
rings in everything
their sons and lovers made

Wind on the winding curve
Tires catch the shoulder, singing
high above the railway
on other roads

Goodbye to the hammer
and the drivingwheel

Margins of passage are narrow
and the forest falls into the streams
forgetting the travellers

And more, and all of these

There is a debt that was cancelled, unpaid

We need more than a railway.
To begin with, gratitude.

The country of the heart
is no place for misers
Nothing that money can buy will pay
its bonds of hope and sorrow

When pride relents, we'll see
what women make is fate
in the night men cling to

Flesh, at the edge of our dreams

IN THE DOME CAR OF THE "CANADIAN"

The mongoloid boy is astounded
with joy at terrific
white-fanged mountains

The shining makes him cry aloud

Tunnels through stone to him
are mysteries, are happy as the womb
And equally happy to him alone
embraced by folly's equanimity
was his birth in this bright world

He claps his hand over his mouth
and moans with ecstasy
to be swallowed whole again
then borne into the glimmering light

These boats along the Fraser
trailing their glistening sweepers
of logs along the river
are arks of all creation
rocking on the dappled water

Oh passengers, you travellers
may strain your eyes to blindness
but never again you'll see
what he is seeing

As he dances in the aisles, for joy

QU'APPELLE

That hill waits in the afternoon
Of the bull with lilac on his breath
It rises, female and rich with flowers
Over the elm and rosebush below

I've heard that hill sigh when the sun
Is up, and seen it undulate
Under a huge bronze tongue

When the clouds come in, and the rain
Bursts down, the hill sinking
Rests, and waits for night
And her other lover the wind

III

The Knife of Love

JACK BE NIMBLE

Nimble would be nicer
Than this constant lifting
If some are born for dancing
Others have to choose

Lightly to our touch
We can feel the pulse
Measuring the song
And we learned to sing
Before we learned to breathe

Who ever thought of failing?

A poet should be thin
To hide behind a word
A woman, or a tree

With diaphragm kept close
To voices felt within
So like a reed it trembles
To inform the tongue

There are no walls like skin
None so exact, or frail

The buzz of being is
Your heart within a finger
Pressed against the thinwalled flower
Tested, on the filed edge
Of a blade

Nimble for ducking
Under the swing
In the playground
Or once I was

Before it clipped me

There's both life and death
After every breath, a voice says

Breathe again
Your candle is still burning

So arguments are small

THE COLOURS

The colours ran together in the heat
I sat around too much, thinking
and my book became a blur
a hectic rainbow

The disjointed days

A boy came and asked me in May
about high water in the mountains
I saw his long limbs in the doorway
and warned him

But a week later,
we pulled his body
out of Stony Creek

On the gravel bar
his shirt was scarlet
his limbs dead white

Then my woman miscarried
and lost our baby
late that summer,
and time drifted crazily
like a kite with a broken string

In the blue wells of her eyes
on the faded roses in her garden
and the bright clothes
unused in her nursery

The colours, the colours!
the bright bars of a cage,
how fast can the heart
beat its wings?

When we woke up,
it was winter

Oh, the healing snow

She and I
we'd had quite enough
of the flowers

LOVE SONG OF THE OVERWEIGHT ANGEL

Twenty thousand sparrows come on in
riding a fading arrow of snow
take rooms in the leafless lilac
to look for seed in the new earth

Cock robin may break his beak
trying to pry worms out of ice
Chirrupping all day in the sun
of spring, but quiet maybe
thoughtful in the cold night
he saves his strength for the ice
this thoroughly Canadian bird

I grow numb like him, with hunger
but my nameless hunger crawls
without an end

Deer-footed grace danced
over my humble hill
and raised in my memory
some furry, secular pang

Given my saintly inclinations
who'd have guessed
that those airy limbs
that cloud of shifting thighs
flashing beneath thin cover
like rabbits through strawberry
gardens of delight
could wield such power
and I'd be torn
by small nails such as these

I, whose skin was hardened
by the humdrum assaults of demons

Oh you horny sparrows
raucous as a Shriner's convention
full with the purblind optimism of sun
you robins with your new bud song
and lovers, having found the one
pretend the season begins with you

Ignore my ordinary fire

I haven't lost love
Only grown numb from wanting more

When Blake wrote "less than all
cannot satisfy man"
poetry's crazy smoke ascended
Now it's the bane of the seraphim, too.
I bawl at the sting
like a calf scorched with an iron

I tell you I'm burning, I'm on fire!
And when she smelt me smouldering
Venus, as a favour from the rival persuasions
had me declared a supernumerary
They said I was too young to be religious
and she, declaring me too fat to be immortal,
sent me to the pyres of romance
to be a jester for the gods

No, I'm not any kind of an angel.
Only a shopworn singer, cooking
with lust again. Writing the aphrodisiac
recipes of the married man. . .

My bags are packed in this strange hotel
I'll sit by the open window in the cold
write poems to the retiring moon
that frigid bitch Diana
and let the wind shake my pages
until it's time to go

Love
I am far away
on the other side of a river
many rivers away

There are mountains standing in between
stretches of prairie flayed by wind
But these barriers are nothing
compared to temptation

My head's a cannonball
heavy with good intentions
So much drag on these wings

That's why I fell so hard
the first time when you said
"Come as you are
I'll take it all"

My bluejeans don't fit
my disguise is wearing thin

It's time to go out
where the black and white spring
is starting its colours
like verbs in a dull page
It's time to get some exercise

Lady, your fervent Icarus is coming home
expecting everything, like Dracula
Applause in hell
and paradise on earth

When for his hesitations
only you can say
what he deserves

O Lady,
see him strain for altitude
a tired buzzard pursued by crows

Only your trust, your love
sustains those rusty wings

Do you hear?
The poor fool can hardly breathe
yet when he catches sight of you
he tries to sing

THE AWAKENING

Out of bed, I fumble in the closet
and your blouse falls against my chest
An unexpected caress

From the languid cloth
that you left on its hanger,
a shadow of yourself

And I wake up standing in our room
Impossible to describe
how large it has grown

A wing of sun glides over the wall

Look out, wherever you are
on the beckoning garden

If you see one red flower
think of me

PRISONER

Whose is the form behind your form
light within light of you
What ripples through
your sleeping limbs

Separate from present and past
Woman, my alien

Who calls out behind your eyes,
in the throes of love
a cry like pain
and is barely glimpsed

Calls out to me, and swiftly goes
leaving us ourselves again

Are you acting, love
betrayed by your eyes, or
have you a prisoner
in disguise

Who is the hostage
in our arms
Who shall we recognize?

THE TOUCH

Tell me, will you bear
half of Genesis in a belly?
What fish skips across my back
when you rest your body
against my spine
The unborn taps against me then
A tide against my bony shore, a questioning

Perhaps a demon
perhaps an angel
but probably an ordinary
miracle, two-thirds immortal
with the fatal third of clay
wrapped in a tent of blood
for prophecy
in the sudden daylight

Tell me what you hear
when you are dreaming
and cry out, is it to me?

I wake, and feel the pulse
fluttering against my palm
held over your burgeoning womb
Your silent answer

It nestles above your proud thighs
when the nights are long

Not that you ever denied me
But who can love his destiny
made manifest, trust the favour
of a captured citadel

You keep our fate.
It sprang from us
a flower from our dying forms
from me to you

The child touches me
in the night, when I can't sleep
and you are lost to dreams
and meetings with a stranger

GRAVITY

After a birth, the body grows toward death

The future sleeps in clothes
or in the toys of children
lined up on a shelf

After a birth
the body keeps itself

The future is the precipice
between us when we kiss
What we have made
but do not know

After a time, the Baby smiles
and wakes us from despair

What can it hope for?

The earth along the shore
where the approaching sea
devours our guarantees

Castles of sand, shells, blood.
This tide is a fist at our hearts.

After a birth, the body grows toward death
And everything we seize
changes in our grip
becomes a circle

Pendant zero, time's vestigial foot
O integer!
How you roll your weary humour
over this world

To move is futile, to stay
impossible. So take my hand
forgive my questions

Life is the argument
that justifies the brain
as we unwind and die
in company
with all the grace we can

Though when we drown
mute fish of dirt and water
expressionless, serene
will eat our furious syllables
down to the round and empty
numerals of our mouths
and make but portals of our dreams

Then, will a note be ringing?
Let nothing break us
We are the wave, and the tide
that emboldens. The gate of Chaos
rests its nervous
volcanic throat in us
and trees root in our fingers

O but we are also the pink
cliché flamingoes in some god's
walled garden

But there's no room for irony
in a lover's thoughts

Until they know
where love will go
and faith can take us

Where roots pulse forward into the earth
space presses on the mind
and gravity delivers the child

THERE JUST AIN'T NO RESPECT

There's a vacuum cleaner
in the middle of the hall,
I whispered icily to her
breathing in the dark bed

Is there? she murmured huskily
hiding her hostility
beneath a fake allure
knowing full well there was

She'd left it there
an act of mutiny
against the pernickety laws
of good housekeeping

Daring me to notice

Well, my leg's in a cast at the time
I'd broken it at work
on avalanche control
(you drop dynamite in snow drifts,
they pay you for this)
I tried to chop down a tree
with my ski, while my foot
was still attached
outrunning an amorous snowslide

So all day I crutch
nimbly over the Electrolux
like a three-legged polevaulter
without complaint
until I gleefully forget the thing is there

All night I lie with ankle throbbing
thinking how Jack Spicer
took liberties with Lorca's poems

and made more
than a simple reproduction
for the English tongue

At four a.m. I get up to stretch
damn thing is killing me
Check the kids' blankets she says
sleepily

Well it's pitch black, in the old rhythm ranch
and my mind's full of wondrous poetry
I hit that vacuum cleaner
waiting in the dark for me
That knobby bowling ball
on its tangled chain
that metal crocodile
with flailing nylon tail

And the song I sang
was the song
of the iron piano

Lorca's poems whiz
right out of my mind
And stars shoot through
a dark red cloud

There just ain't no respect
for poets, in this world
or the next

I cut my toe. . .
I'm tracking blood on the cold floor
but I don't cry out, being
a hardened husband
Just
cover the babies
my teeth clenched
and limp back to bed

To hiss at her
who huddles by the wall
There's
a vacuum cleaner
in the middle of the hall

To which she answers, triumphantly
I know.
Whew! Your feet are cold

I lie there, feeling like dead Lorca
executed by machinery he didn't recognize
Or in my case, the merely homicidal mate

Remembering the folly
of dancing on my cast
while drunk, to demonstrate
the cripple's two step

Breaking the thing in mid-caper
(soaked as it was, with spilt rum)
So a nurse, white as death
had to cut it off
with a powersaw, her tight smile
promised cancer of the anklebone

I'm wide awake, for sure.
That flower of womanhood
she lies in the dark, asleep
I can hear her gently breathe

The scent of her is all
rose petals and morphine dream

I move that way
Arms and legs surround me
warmth dissolves the pain
slowly
        into
                sleep, and

here comes the ghost of Spicer
chasing me with a vacuum cleaner that's
spouting an avalanche of poems

Hovering and Hoovering

Lorca!
Damn it all. Lorca,
stop laughing at my metaphors. . .

FATHERHOOD

They nudge us into the past
when the baby's born
as if they'd grown afraid of us
male animals
with long teeth

If we come to their miracle
with gifts and tenderness
we're still but adjuncts to the breast
They'll love us, and disguise contempt

But never love us as before
rolling wild before the fire
with wine in the mouth
and leaves in their hair

Now with the sweet smiles of martyrs
they view our fishing trips
our books and bottles
our spectator accomplishments

They close their thighs more often
and we learn, pleasure is its own betrayal
Love is an ambush planned by cells
Each sex dwells in a separate tense

Baby is the present idol
heaped with sacrifice
A whole life festooned
around its tiny shoulders

But soon the idol wakens
with an ego, an opposing mind

Another betrayal, a final pain.

Women without men, still have their children
or else their projects, their coffee cups, careers.

A sense of righteousness.

And when their babies leave them,
when they have outlived their expectations

They'll have themselves, and memory.

It's more than for the love
of flesh and blood
we learn to be good fathers
study gentleness
strive to oppose
the hunter in our veins

It's towards a new communing
this yearning
To take our place again
when they remember us

The women that we love

LIVING WITHOUT YOU

Living without you becomes
part of a dying motion
foregone conclusions of the body
in which the soul still struggles
A hawk, beneath its hood

Today I pushed through miles of air
running on cross country skis
toward you, days away
through westerly snows

Trying to exhaust desire
running through the jackpine and poplar

Through the slush of two lakes, the crust
rotten with spring heat
collapsed as I stepped out
like the parchment of a broken drum
Rattling and booming all the way
to the far shore

Falling onto the ice below, it held
but coming back I went through
in such cold water!

Yet nothing cools this heat
Not icewater, distance or time

Listen. The whole land is a body
I've wrestled with all afternoon
You've heard that line before
You think that I mean yours;
I do. A female body.
My eyes have raped my mind

And I'd pull off this hood
If I remembered
how to fly

This is what your love has done
to me, this is the hunger
that drives me through the snow
engraving the country
with sharp signatures of possession
though they melt in the heat of the sun

It brings me here, with hands
that reach blind into distance
to punch it out of my way

To cut a road through winter
that the sun will leave standing a while
in bas relief
on the green mirrors of its largesse

The tracks of the wolves desert me
at the edge of your unmarked plain

I am the last of your hunters.
Lie to me, tell me you are gone
are not here, beneath my wings

The hawk beneath its hood
is sure of the hawker's voice, the law.
It feels the fist clench in its claws
Remembers feathers, caught by sun
Red fires that slaked, in fur

Then, when the jesses strain
it spreads its silent beak
in darkness, wills its heart

Be still.
Listen.
The hollow drums of spring
are beating on the lakes

Time falls away from us
like an old skin

THE KNIFE OF LOVE

On the day before my birthday
a message comes unbidden
in the form of a long forgotten scent,
a front porch smell of fresh paint
and sun splashed cottonwoods

Grandmother's. In one corner
in an old cane chair
playing with the doorstop
a time-coloured glass insulator
is a small boy

My grandparents are dead
quilted under the sod
my grandfather broke, yet
could not subdue. But the message
comes over the prairie and over
the mountains, the hundred valleys
comes up the invisible wire of memory
to a cabin on Bryant Creek
where my hand curls the remembered glass
behind log walls

And the elk in the meadow lift their heads
startled from the strawberry leaves
hearing on my lips, a cry

I see the dim light through a blur of tears
and feel a pressure in my throat
That waking of grief like a knife
or the arm, say, of your lover
abandoned in sleep, flung across your neck

The knife of love will pierce you then
Kiss it gently
and move it from your breath, or try

That day alone, the open door
Wind that stirs the breakfast fire
Cold food that I push aside
ashamed of hunger, to grieve

For an ex-Montana sheriff
and a plump Dutch wife who tried
Beuhla land with eight kids and a rusty plough
who never found the time to say "I love you"
to anyone or anything, who acted like the verb
was too luxurious to utter
against the long noun of work
and eight imperatives of pain

I'll spell it for them now, in this morning hour
Even in those crystal moments on the porch
I was learning to forget them, blind
to anything but words

I ate their food, slept in their house
and went away like a season

Being abandoned by the leaves and flowers
was nothing new to them. But it made them hard
and in the end, it drove them apart
like a wedge in a poplar stump

They were bitter when they died

I'll spell it for them now, for the boy alone
for the turning wind — for those two who found
the time too late for the wrong reason
For anyone who holds a puzzle in his hand

Who, looking in enchanted turns inward
until the world can't touch him any more

The cabin was too dark
I walked outside, but the depth
of it preceded me as if the night
was carried in my body like a wound

A morning in the veins eclipses dawn
in the waking, when all waking's done

And wellings! I had never known
the tongue in me
was one bright spear
poised upon the fulcrum of that word
a balance tipping in my ears
as I walked out, took
one step, two
and stopped.

My plumbob heart, dangling
hooked to time
trembled in its brief
relentless evening

Then I saw Mount Eon

      ten
    thousand
   f e   e t
  h   i   g   h

Today it looks no bigger than a tombstone

While leaning on his marker
God or a cloud or
the Man who died

Watching me to see
if I had the message
before he plucked his brilliant
sliver from my throat

And sent it glimmering toward the sun

REVELATION

I held our new baby
against my bare chest
and his four-day-old mouth
explored my tingling skin

Until he found a nipple
my milkless, small
and hairy nipple

He battened on

It was a major disappointment
for both of us

TURNING TO MEET THE WORLD

Small foot of my son
a pink, warm mammal
wriggles in my palm
loving the field of flesh
contending, but struggling
to be released as well

For too long
I have dodged the world
placing a screen of trees
and rock along my path

I've made a world of my own
in the palm of a mountain

Doubling on the hunters,
I've left them in front of me
until I left them behind

They were blind to mountains
All they saw was their ambition's scenery
They'll kill themselves
but they won't kill me

The valley narrows now
the walls grow high

If this is the last mountain
I ever climb,
what of it?

There are other ranges, shining
blue and bright
in a boy's eye

OUR DAILY DEATH

Sleep against my shoulder
I may give unwieldy comfort
If bulky I'm warm blooded
And you can bed against me
like a deer below a hill
I would be stronger
and more tangible still
be sun heated rock, for you

No one understands this life,
some pretend to know
It will evolve without us
abandoned to its chimeras at night

Try to imagine
that we're living while we sleep
our daily death
We must forgive ourselves
our disbelief
and no one else

Someone is awake to see
stars don't move to other heavens
while you sleep

It is a different thing
I mean, not God
but living company
The kind that a tired creature
gives to the roots of a rough-barked tree

So sleep now, turning
as the small planet spins

I swore to believe
in things that I could touch
but love is only trust
So I'll believe in you
journeying far away from me
yet growing ever near

FOR MY SONS

Two boys in my lap,
and I've become a horse
a swing, a raft on a creek,
the strong limb of a tree
poised over a hay stack

Sitting at my poems
trying to engage the imagination
as they crawled up my chair
and made me
a creature of theirs

MR. PORCUPINE
for Paul and Buck

Why am I so impatient with you?
My father's voice is trapped in me,
too abruptly
goes on listing your jejune sins
I'd best be gentle
or I'll breed these barbs
from your thin skin

It's like carping at a tree
because its branches scratch my face
rebuking the wind
for you're an element like these

Little one. You must forgive a father
shouting down a boy's unhappiness
denying its reality

Forgive my lapsing memory
of childhood

I live too far up
in your sky of love and fear

Why can't I know it,
and believe
how you're convinced that I
can throw the thunder around

For I must bend
to see your tears
to realize, I'm good enough
at last. Better than I'd hoped
to be: am all, to you.

That's hard for me, you know.
To be your hero,

though I'll try
I'm young enough to play
the role
but I'm too old to lie

A few more years,
you'll be ashamed of tears
and learn the sins of pride

Then, these, wetting my proffered hand
burning me with their warmth
will be forever dry

When your face becomes
my mirror
when your eyes have learned
to weigh me

Father rival

I pick you up, hear you cry
with glee now, at my hedgehog whiskers
on your tender chin
already, smiling through your tears

Such bravery!

Love has quills, like a porcupine
like the flower in the thorns

Most men embrace too carefully
afraid of being hurt, afraid of hurting

But you and I, we'll never be
so let me squeeze you now
and you squeeze me

A porcupine no more:
I'll be your bear.

Though my rough skin stings yours
in our arms' clinging
treading round our dance

There is pain, in love
In indifference, worse

And that's one pain
I swear
you'll never get from me

THE BETRAYAL

The pig was happy, proud and fat
I decoyed him with a pail of chop
to the edge of the pen

Uncle Biff leaned close with his .22
and as the pig bent, greedily
joyfully to eat
shot him once between the eyes

The pig backed up fast, terribly surprised
His small eyes turned inward — too late,
following the passage of lead through his brain
and before they could start to open out again
to us; squeezed shut

Biff was quick with the long knife. Truly
the pig had felt no pain
had died without the squealing fear
and death smell of the abattoir.
The other pigs made no objection, either.
They sniffed the victim over, then
satisfied, hurried back to their trough

But my little sons had seen it all
(I'd tried, but could not keep them back)
and they were very quiet after that
Polite, when we gave them food
said "Thank you" very carefully, for days.

THE FORDING

A woman and a boy ride down into Bryant Creek
They water their horses at the ford
under the glacier brow of Mount Eon

My woman and my son, strangers in weathered hats
sit their horses and talk in the middle of the stream
of the things that beautiful women and small boys
talk of, there where the wind blows the first buds
of the cinquefoil, and trout skip forward
from the billowing mud under a horse's foot
to glitter in the clear again

I would be like those quick gleams
to be always shining for their eyes and hearts.
A selfish man. But I can't help longing
to be held with them in their perfect moment
needed to frame this day, as they frame mine

How their yellow slickers trail along the wind!
I watch and build an answering fire
here at the clearing's edge.

They turn toward the smoke and canter
my living lights, the fire of my days.
Shining motes are we, below the massed green timber

With a whoop, with a shout
they are riding toward me now
Smashing the dewy alder shrubs to rainbows
over a plain of trembling orange flowers
making me cry aloud at their fatal beauty
Go running forward to meet them, and surrender

ACKNOWLEDGEMENTS

Some of these poems have appeared in the following magazines:

The Canadian Forum; The Newest Review; The Capilano Review; The Windsor Lance; Anthracite Chronicle; Arc 1; Sundog; Repository.
All the poems have been revised since publication above.

I would like to thank the Peter and Catherine Whyte Foundation of Banff for providing me with working space, and the Canada Council for a short-term grant. Thanks to John Newlove for his critical eye, and to Al and Eurithe Purdy for reality sandwiches and fiddlehead greens.